FAMILIES

THE WORLD OF ART

FAMILIES

through the eyes of artists

Wendy & Jack Richardson

CHILDRENS PRESS ®
CHICAGO

Originally published by Macmillan Publishers Ltd 1989
© Heinemann Children's Reference 1990

Picture research by Faith Perkins

Printed in Italy

Library of Congress Cataloging-in-Publication Data

Richardson, Wendy
    Families: through the eyes of artists/ by Wendy and Jack
        Richardson. p.   cm. – (The World of art)
    Reprint. Originally published: Houndmills, Basingstoke,
Hampshire: Macmillan, 1989.
    Summary: Presents paintings and drawings of family life by
notable artists. Includes descriptive material about each artist and
the accompanying work.
    ISBN 0-516-09284-7
    1. Family in art – Juvenile literature. 2. Art – Juvenile literature.
[1. Family in art. 2. Art. 3. Art appreciation.]
I. Richardson, Jack, 1940-   . II. Title. III. Series: Richardson,
Wendy. World of art.
N8217.F27R6 1990
758′.930685–dc20   90-34279
                                                              CIP
                                                              AC

Photographic acknowledgments
The authors and publishers wish to acknowledge with thanks the following photographic sources:

Cover: Père Juniet's Cart – Musée de l'Orangerie, Paris (The Bridgeman Art Library)

Family on the Beach (Picasso) © The Pace Gallery 1986 (Photo courtesy of the Atlantic Monthly Press), 3
Berthe Morisot – Private Collection (Giraudon), 6
Gauguin – National Gallery of Art, Washington, D.C. The Chester Dale Collection, 8
Where Do We Come From? What Are We? Where Are We Going? – The Museum of Fine Arts, Boston. Tompkins Collection. Purchase, Arthur Gordon Tompkins Fund, 9
Berthe Morisot – Private Collection (Giraudon), 10
The Cradle – Musée D'Orsay, Paris (Bulloz), 11
Raphael – Uffizi, Florence (Scala), 12
Madonna and Child – Reproduced by courtesy of the Trustees of The British Museum, 12
Leonardo da Vinci – Windsor Castle, Royal Library © Her Majesty The Queen, 12
The Virgin and Child with St. Anne and John the Baptist – The National Gallery, London, 13
Rembrandt – The Iveagh Bequest, Kenwood, London (English Heritage), 14

Holy Family with Angels – The Hermitage, Leningrad (The Bridgeman Art Library), 15
The Flight – (Visual Publication Ltd), 17
Van Gogh – The Metropolitan Museum of Art, New York, Bequest Miss Adelaide Milton de Groot, 1967, 18
The First Steps – The Metropolitan Museum of Art, New York, Gi of George N. and Helen M. Richard, 1964, 19
Welcome and Many Happy Returns to a Grandson – (Aurora A Publishers USSR), 21
Valadon – Glyptothek, Copenhagen (The Bridgeman Art Library), 22
Dressing Two Children in the Garden – The Fine Arts Museum of San Francisco. M. H. De Young Memorial Museum, 23
Gainsborough – The National Portrait Gallery, London, 24
The Painter's Daughters with a Cat – The National Gallery, London, 25
Chagall – Kunstsammlung, Dusseldorf © ADAGP, Paris/DACS, London 1988, 26
Bride with a Fan – Private Collection © ADAGP, Paris/DACS, London 1988, 27
Beryl Cook – © Beryl Cook (Photograph Rogers, Coleridge, and White Ltd), 28
Wedding Photograph © Beryl Cook (Photograph Rogers, Coleridge, and White), 29
John Everett Millais – The National Portrait Gallery, London, 30
The Order of Release – The Tate Gallery, London, 31
Frans Hals – The Metropolitan Museum of Art, New York, Beques of Michael Friedsam, 1931. The Friedsam Collection, 32
A Family Group in a Landscape – The National Gallery, London, 33
Lowry – Salford Art Gallery and Museum. Reproduced by courtes of Mrs Carol Ann Danes (The Bridgeman Art Library), 34
On the Promenade – Roy Miles Fine Paintings, London. Reproduced by courtesy of Mrs Carol Ann Danes (The Bridgeman Art Library), 35
Rousseau – Narodini Gallery, Prague (The Bridgeman Art Library), 36
Père Juniet's Cart – Musée de l'Orangerie, Paris (The Bridgeman Art Library), 37
Velázquez – The Prado, Madrid (Scala), 38
An Old Woman Cooking Eggs – National Gallery of Scotland, Edinburgh (The Bridgeman Art Library), 39
A Funeral – Statens Museum for Kunst, Copenhagen. (Photograp Hans Petersen), 41
Munch – Nasjonalgalleriet, Oslo, 42
By the Death Bed – Oslo Kommunes Kunstsamlinger, Munch-Museet, 43
Ensor – Stadsbestur, Ostend © ADAGP, Paris/DACS, London 1988, 44
The Artist's Mother in Death – Stadsbestur, Ostend © ADAGP, Paris/DACS, London 1988, 45
Stanley Spencer – The Tate Gallery, London, 46
The Resurrection: Reunion of Families – Dundee Art Galleries and Museums, 47

Introduction

This is a book of pictures about family life. Some of the paintings are old, and some were painted quite recently. Some are in books, some are drawings, and some are paintings. They come from many different parts of the world. They all look different but they have one thing in common. They were made by people who had an idea about family life and thought that the best way to share the idea was through a picture. So this is a book for you to look at.

The pictures tell how the artists feel about some of the important moments in family life. All the members of the family are here, singly or in groups, as babies and children, as parents and grandparents. The happy moments and the sad moments are here. Families of all sorts, doing special things or everyday things, are here for you to see. Look closely at the pictures to see if you can find out what the painters hoped to tell us through their work.

manet 7[...]

Contents

Where Do We Come From? What Are We? Where Are We Going?

Oil on canvas 4'3¼" × 12'3½"

Paul Gauguin

LIVED:
1848-1903

NATIONALITY:
French

TYPE OF WORK:
oil paintings, ceramics, sculpture, woodcut prints

National Gallery of Art, Washington, D.C. The Chester Dale Collection

Paul Gauguin became interested in art and began painting when he came to Paris. Gauguin was among the first European artists to be interested in art that came from outside Europe, and in 1891, he left France for Tahiti. His boyhood in Peru had given him a taste for exciting new places. Gauguin longed to express himself in a way that was simple, direct, and strong.

Surpassing all

This painting is probably Gauguin's most famous work, and also his largest. Gauguin described it himself in a letter to his friend and fellow artist, Daniel de Monfried, "I wanted, before dying, to paint a great canvas that I had in mind, and for the whole month I worked day and night in an unprecedented fever . . . It is all dashed off with the tip of the brush on burlap,* full of knots and wrinkles so that its appearance is terribly rough . . . I think that this canvas not only surpasses in merit all the preceding ones, but even that I will never do a better or a similar one . . ."

Expressive color

Gauguin used color to describe feelings, or for its decorative effect, rather than to show how things actually look. He tells his friend in the letter, "The two upper corners are chrome yellow . . . like a fresco damaged in the corners, applied on to a gold wall . . . the appearance of the landscape is consistently blue and Veronese green from end to end. Against that all the nude figures stand out in bold orange."

Symbols for life

Each part of the painting had a meaning. "The idol . . . seems to point to the hereafter . . . a crouching figure seems to listen to the idol . . . an old woman near death seems to accept, to resign herself . . . at her feet a strange white bird holding a lizard in its foot represents the uselessness of idle words." Gauguin simplified the outlines of his shapes, and used large blocks of flat color in his pictures. His work seemed savage and primitive to Europeans.

* burlap: a coarse fabric, used for wall covering or wrapping

The Museum of Fine Arts, Boston. Tompkins Collection. Purchase, Arthur Gordon Tompkins Fund

The Cradle

Oil on canvas 1'9¾" × 1'6"
Berthe Morisot

LIVED:
1841-1895

NATIONALITY:
French

TYPE OF WORK:
oil and watercolor paintings

Private Collection

Berthe Morisot was one of three daughters in a wealthy French family. Berthe and her sister Edma were encouraged by their parents to develop their talent for painting. One of their teachers persuaded the young artists to work outdoors, in natural light, looking directly at nature. This was to have a strong influence on Morisot's later work.

Supporting the impressionists

In 1868 Morisot met the painter Manet. They became life-long friends and were strong influences on each other's work. Morisot later married Manet's brother. She also met Monet and Renoir who were members of the group to become known as the impressionists. She understood what they were trying to do and, like them, she tried to represent what the eye could actually see. She liked the way they dealt with light and liked their use of the paint, placing colors next to each other in patches rather than mixing them on the palette. The art critics and dealers, however, could see no merit in the new style of painting. Morisot, who was already accepted in the established painting world, joined the impressionists and exhibited with them in their annual shows. It was courageous of her to support them, because she had no need to prove herself to the art critics of the time. The impressionists were once described as "five or six lunatics, one of whom is a woman."

An interest in people

This painting is a portrait of Edma, who had given up painting when she married. It was done the year before the first impressionist exhibition and was praised by the art critics. Morisot and Renoir were the only painters in the group to show a real interest in painting people. This picture shows that while Morisot is starting to use paint in an impressionistic manner, she is also concerned with the feeling of the painting. The mother looks at her child with a quiet devotion as the baby sleeps. Her hand holds the gauze canopy as she rests on one elbow, just looking at her child.

Morisot also painted bright shimmering landscapes, but it is her portraits and pictures of women and children that show her real strengths as a painter.

Madonna and Child

Black chalk on greenish-grey paper, originally blue 1'3¾" × 10½"

Raffaello Sanzio (known as Raphael)

LIVED:
1483-1520

NATIONALITY:
Italian

TYPE OF WORK:
paintings and architecture

The Virgin and Child with St. Anne and John the Baptis

Black and white chalks on paper 4'7½" × 3'5¼"

Leonardo da Vinci

LIVED:
1452-1519

NATIONALITY:
Italian

TYPE OF WORK:
paintings, architecture, engineerir
music

Michelangelo, Leonardo da Vinci, and Raphael stand together as the finest painters and draftsmen of the Italian Renaissance, the time when there was a rebirth of interest in Greek and Roman art.

The young genius

The three painters knew each other well and Raphael, the youngest man, was certainly influenced by the other two. He worked in Florence for a time, where the two older men were working, learning all he could from them. When he moved to Rome, he quickly became so famous that he could not complete all the work that was demanded of him. He painted frescoes and portraits as well as pictures with a religious theme. He designed buildings and completed large murals. Raphael died when he was only thirty-seven, leaving behind a vast number of wall paintings, portraits, and altar paintings. Most of his buildings have been altered beyond recognition but we still have many of his wonderful paintings.

The thinker

Leonardo da Vinci was an extraordinary man. He was a scientist, experimenting with flight among other things. He had a keen interest in natural history and filled book after book with drawings. He designed weapons. He was an accomplished musician and he was a wonderful painter and draftsman. He was also a great thinker, and it is due to him that the idea of a painter as a creative thinker, and not just as a skilled craftworker, was born. Unfortunately, he was often more interested in figuring out how to do something than in getting down to work and finishing it! Much of his painting is incomplete.

The Holy Family

Here we see drawings by two of the great three, who all painted the Holy Family, the central figures of the Christian faith, many times. Both drawings show the Virgin Mary and Jesus, but Leonardo has brought other figures into the group and has woven them all into one tight mass. How do you think the drawings compare? Were the artists trying to express the same ideas? How similar do you think the drawings are? What are the differences?

The Holy Family with Angels

Oil on canvas 3'10" × 3'11¾"

Rembrandt van Rijn

LIVED:
1606-1669

NATIONALITY:
Dutch

TYPE OF WORK:
paintings, drawings, prints

The Iveagh Bequest, Kenwood, London

Rembrandt van Rijn was a successful and popular painter in his lifetime and is thought of today in the same class as Leonardo, Michelangelo, and Raphael. He was a very skilled graphic artist and a superb portrait painter. He painted wonderful landscapes and intense, emotional religious paintings.

Rembrandt was apprenticed as a painter after a short time at the University of Leiden in what is now The Netherlands. He learned the techniques and skills of painting and became an accomplished craftsman. But it is as an expressive painter of people that Rembrandt is best known. He earned a good living painting portraits of dignitaries, but he did not make his subjects look grand or important. He painted them honestly, as he saw them, and we see their characters too. Rembrandt was equally honest about himself. He painted self-portraits throughout his life, leaving us a record of himself.

The ordinary Holy Family

Rembrandt's favorite work was the retelling in picture form of stories from the Bible. In this picture, Rembrandt has combined his skill in handling the paint with his understanding of people and produced a quiet and ordinary Holy Family. Joseph, painted entirely in brown, is a shadowy figure in his living-working room. He works away as his wife reads, keeps her feet warm, and cares for their son. She, a very young Mary, peeps into the cradle to check that the child still sleeps. Her face hints of her pride and pleasure. All is well. She moves the green cover carefully so that the baby's face remains shaded. He is tranquil in the deep sleep of little children. His chubby hand is relaxed upon the sheets.

No one would suspect that this is a special family if it were not for the little angels hovering over the child. It is from them that the light falls onto Mary's book, and against their light that she has draped the protective cloth. They light her face so that we can see her tender expression. It is as if she is used to their presence guarding her son, symbolizing his extraordinary being.

Compare the two drawings of Leonardo and Raphael with the painting of Rembrandt. Can you detect differences in their feelings about these central figures in Christianity?

The Flight

Oil on canvas 4' × 4'
Yusuf Grillo

BORN:
1934

NATIONALITY:
Nigerian

TYPE OF WORK:
paintings

Yusuf Grillo was trained as a painter at Yaba College of Technology in Nigeria, where he now heads the Art and Printing Department. He was also a student at the University of Zaria. He is one of many African artists whose painting style fuses the traditions of Africa with the painting of twentieth-century Europe. It was from Africa that several of the young European painters of the early twentieth century drew their inspiration.

Crossing boundaries

This painting is of Mary, Joseph, and Jesus fleeing from King Herod to safety in Egypt. Mary is dressed in the blue that has become traditional, but so is Joseph. Blue and green are the colors preferred by Grillo and he has frequently painted whole pictures using only these colors. This painting is composed of large, curving areas of color outlined in black. The effect is rather like a stained-glass window. The forest is suggested in the green behind the travelers, the sky is blue behind the trees.

A story for the world

Mary, seated on the crossbar of a bicycle rather than on a donkey, looks down tenderly at the baby she holds. Joseph is expecting to be away for some time. He has brought his tools with him so that he can earn a living. Grillo has painted a twentieth-century family and, being an African, he has painted an African family. Rembrandt painted his Holy Family in a seventeenth-century setting, so Grillo was not being revolutionary when he painted the family in a modern setting. His painting reminds Christians that Jesus was sent to bring help to all the peoples of the world. Christians believe that his help is as available today as it was 2,000 years ago.

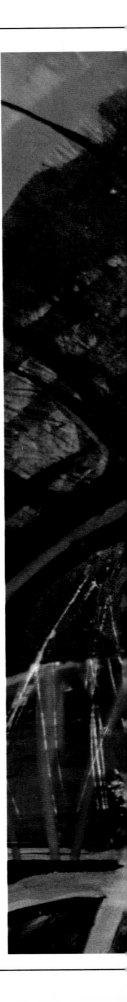

The First Steps

Oil on canvas 2'4¾" × 3'0¼"

Vincent van Gogh

LIVED:
1853-1890

NATIONALITY:
Dutch

TYPE OF WORK:
drawings, oil paintings

The Metropolitan Museum of Art, New York.
Bequest of Miss Adelaide Milton de Groot, 1967

A picture by Vincent van Gogh was sold at auction in November 1987 for $53.9 million. The sale highlights the tragedy of the life of the man who painted it. He sold only one of his paintings during his lifetime. His work was much admired by fellow painters but did not appeal to the critics or to the public. He spent months at a time in an asylum, suffering from attacks of very serious mental illness. At the age of thirty-seven, he shot himself in the chest and died two days later.

A strong influence

Van Gogh started work as a young man in an art dealer's gallery. He knew the work of all the artists of his time. He was a very great admirer of Jean-François Millet, a French painter who died a few years before van Gogh started painting. Van Gogh, a religious man who had been a lay preacher, was impressed by the social message in Millet's work. He often chose the same subject matter as Millet, painting peasants working in the fields and simple, unromantic landscapes. Several times he made copies of Millet's pictures. Van Gogh himself received little training. He was largely self-taught. Like Gauguin, he wanted his paintings to speak for themselves.

One painter through another

This picture, painted a few months before van Gogh's death, shows him once more turning to Millet for inspiration. He has painted a peasant family in a simple everyday scene. A little child takes its first steps toward the outstretched arms of its father. We see both painters at once, one through the other. The brushwork and thick swirling marks and the color are unmistakably van Gogh. The figures, particularly the straight-backed woman leaning over her child, are Millet's. The country scene that the figures inhabit belongs to both painters.

When he saw some pastel drawings by Millet, van Gogh said that he felt he ought to take off his shoes as he stood before them, as if he were in a sacred place. It would be interesting to know what Millet might have thought of his disciple had he lived to see van Gogh's work.

The Metropolitan Museum of Art, New York. Gift of George N. and Helen M. Richard, 1964

Welcome and Many Happy Returns to a Grandson

Tempera and oil on canvas 5'5" × 6'6¾"

Vladimir Mikita

BORN:
1931

NATIONALITY:
Russian

TYPE OF WORK:
oil paintings

Vladimir Vasillevich Mikita is a Russian painter from an area called Transcarpathia. He paints portraits and landscapes and pictures like this one, showing scenes from the life of the Russian villagers among whom he lives.

This painting records a special family occasion. The whole village has gathered together in the village hall to celebrate the birth of a new baby. The chairs have been pushed to one side, and everyone who can get on the floor is on their feet in a swirling dance. The people are dressed in traditional costume, the women wear headscarves and everyone has big warm boots of fur or felt. They are warmly dressed even for this occasion. The proud parents sit at the back of the hall. The mother holds the baby. Those who cannot find room to join in sit at the side of the room chatting to their friends. The old men sit together and share the fun.

Visual rhythm

The picture is full of exciting movement. Mikita has made a stong rhythmical pattern of the repeated groups of dancers and the interwoven colors of the men's and women's jackets. The soft beiges and purplish browns and the blues of the swirling skirts are set off by the orange dots of the headscarves. Near the center is one green headscarf. Try blotting it out with your finger and see what an important part that one spot of color plays.

Just as painters do everywhere, Mikita works from real life. The people here are his friends and neighbors. They appear in many of his works.

Dressing Two Children in the Garden

Drypoint on paper 1' 1¼" × 1' 3⅓"

Suzanne Valadon

LIVED:
1867-1938

NATIONALITY:
French

TYPE OF WORK:
mainly figure painting

Glyptothek, Copenhagen

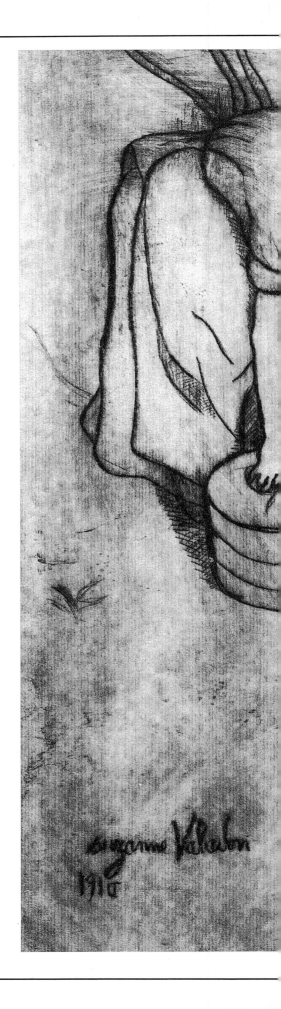

Suzanne Valadon was a very determined character. As a young woman she worked as an acrobat, but a fall from a trapeze ended her circus career. She then found work as an artist's model. She said that from the very first day she posed she knew that she was in the right place. She felt at home in the studio and knew that she would never go away from art. She taught herself to paint and was encouraged by several of the painters for whom she sat. Degas and Toulouse-Lautrec were among the first to recognize her talent.

A strong woman with a strong style

Valadon developed a strong and distinct style and mainly painted people. She was probably the first woman to paint the male nude. She painted portraits and did flower paintings. She taught her son, Maurice Utrillo, to paint. Together they sold enough work to lead a comfortable life despite Valadon's extravagance. She was known to feed caviar to her cats.

Drawing on metal

This little black-and-white picture is a type of engraving known as drypoint. The picture is scratched on a sheet of copper. The sharp point raises a little wall along the edge of the line. This keeps the ink in the line when the plate is wiped off. The point is hard to control on the metal and has to be pushed with some force. This gives work in drypoint a strength and simplicity, as fussy detail is usually left out. Drypoint has a thicker, slightly blurrier line than etching, where the lines are cut with acid.

A strong line

Drypoint suits Valadon's way of working. In color she was bold and lively and gave her paintings strong outlines. Here we see the same strength in the lines. There is no harshness though. It is a gentle family scene. The boy leans cozily on his mother while she puts on his socks. The little girl stands awkwardly, reaching over her shoulder to fasten her dress. The woman in the apron, perhaps a servant, leans on the tub as she empties the water from the summer bath in the garden.

The Painter's Daughters with a Cat

Oil on canvas 2'6" × 2'

Thomas Gainsborough

LIVED:
1727-1788

NATIONALITY:
British

TYPE OF WORK:
paintings and drawings, mainly portraits and landscapes

The National Portrait Gallery, London

Thomas Gainsborough was a popular and successful portrait painter. He painted the rich and the aristocratic and was a favorite of the royal family. Gainsborough was famous for his brilliant brushwork and his lively, fleeting color. He said that he preferred to paint landscapes but the portraits he painted to earn a living show a real interest in his subjects. He paints in a direct, informal way. His subjects do not seem posed, but rather caught for a moment.

A real family portrait

Here we see a double portrait of Gainsborough's daughters. Mary was then aged eleven, and Margaret aged seven. He has painted the girls with their cat. Only their faces are completely finished. Their clothing, the sky behind them, and the trees roughly suggested on either side make a setting for the faces. The sunlight catching the clouds behind their heads gives them a bright halo. The cat was never finished either and appears as a rather ghostly figure in the girls' arms. What color do you think Gainsborough would have painted it if he had finished it? Should it be light or dark to keep the picture balanced?

With his own daughters, whom he obviously knew well, Gainsborough can really show us their characters. Although the girls' features and coloring are similar, they look as if they have quite different personalities. What sort of girls do you think they are? They are not dressed up to have their picture painted, they look as if they have just come in from playing in the garden. They do not look as if they have been standing still for long. The picture has an instant look – as if at any minute the children might run off to continue their game. Even in his formal portraits, Gainsborough often managed to paint so that his subject appeared to be passing through the canvas on the way to somewhere else.

Suggested details

Gainsborough used his brushes in a very loose, free way, often doing no more than suggesting a bit of lace on a cuff or the shine of silk on a sleeve. Unlike other portrait painters who employed assistants to finish work for them, Gainsborough always completed his paintings himself.

The National Gallery, London

Bride with a Fan

Oil on canvas 1'6" × 1'3"

Marc Chagall

LIVED:
1887-1985

NATIONALITY:
born in Russia, became a French citizen in 1937

TYPE OF WORK:
paintings, stained-glass windows, theater design

Kunstsammlung, Dusseldorf © ADAGP, Paris/DACS, London 1988

Marc Chagall, called Moses by his Russian-Jewish parents, was a man very much concerned with love. He said that true art was to be found in love. He thought of love as inspiring his work, choosing his colors, filling him with ideas. He painted every sort of love – romantic love, the love of parents for their children, the love of God, the love of friends, the love of nature. Chagall lived to be almost one hundred years old, and he continued to work until he was over ninety. He painted murals, designed tapestries, and made mosaics and stained-glass windows as well as painting pictures, making lithographs, illustrating books and designing stage sets. His work may be seen in places as far apart as Chichester Cathedral in England, Israel's Knesset Building in Jerusalem, and the United Nations Building in New York City.

Fantasies in brilliant color

Chagall's pictures are brilliant fantasies and at the same time they are reality. They are full of life and energy. They tell stories old and new. They show us a world of make-believe in which we can see a truth that is both beautiful and ugly.

They combine Russian folklore, Jewish stories, Christian beliefs, everyday objects, people, animals, flowers, plants, and places. Put together, they make mysterious, magical, joyful pictures. Colors and objects have their own meanings in Chagall's work.

No explanations

Chagall refused to explain his pictures. He said that each of us could look at them in our own way, deciding for ourselves what we saw and how we saw it. He certainly did not want anyone else to explain his work for him. So the best thing you can do is look at the picture and figure out for yourself what it is about. We will each decide differently. Each part will mean something special to each of us, depending on our own experiences. What can you see in the *Bride with a Fan*?

m Chagall 1911.

Wedding Photograph

Oil on wood

Beryl Cook

© Beryl Cook

BORN:
1928

NATIONALITY:
British

TYPE OF WORK:
oil paintings

Beryl Cook started to paint when she was showing her son how to use his paint box. She found that she was enjoying painting more than he was! Once she started she could not stop. She paints on driftwood from the beach and on scraps from the local lumber yard. She paints people doing everyday things, people in the streets and stores, or in the park or the pub. Some of the people are her friends, and some are people she sees just once.

Beryl Cook has developed a style of her own that shows more than anything else how much she enjoys people and loves life, seeing the funny side in almost any situation. She is very observant of the way people stand and hold their hands. She says she is fond of large hands. She also likes the way people wear their clothes, especially when they are dressed up for special occasions.

A beautiful vision

Cook is a very popular and successful painter, but she finds it hard to get her pictures the way she wants them. She has written of the disappointment that she often feels when paintings do not match up to her "beautiful vision" but says that if she keeps them for a while she comes to accept them for what they are and feels glad that she was able to paint them at all. Then she finds that she misses them when they are sold.

She sometimes adds odd bits and pieces to her paintings, or cuts pictures from magazines and newspapers to stick on them. She collects junk that might one day be useful from fleamarkets and garage sales.

Finding inspiration around her

This painting was inspired by a photograph of a wedding in the local newspaper. She loves large people and often exaggerates the size of people she paints. She says she had been looking for a reason to paint a really large family when she found this photo. Though she does exaggerate, it is never meant to be unkind. She is as able to laugh at herself, as you can see from her portrait (above), as much as she laughs at other people.

© Beryl Cook

The Order of Release

Oil on canvas 3'4½" × 2'5"

John Everett Millais

LIVED:
1829-1896

NATIONALITY:
British

TYPE OF WORK:
paintings and drawings

The National Portrait Gallery, London

John Everett Millais was, at eleven years old, the youngest student ever to attend the Royal Academy of Art in London. There he met Holman Hunt and Rossetti and with them formed a new movement called the Pre-Raphaelite Brotherhood. They painted directly from nature, paying attention to detail and using natural objects in their pictures as symbols of ideas. Their work was not popular at first, but later Millais achieved great popularity.

Popular but true to himself

Critics have sometimes said that Millais wasted his wonderful talent as a painter by seeking popular subjects that would earn money. However, he stuck to his ways of painting no matter what the subject. Millais always painted from nature. When he first had the idea for this painting, he searched for a prison gate or door that would serve as his background. Then he worked with a number of models for each part of the picture. He wrote of the trouble he had keeping the child and the dog from moving. He used models to paint the hands that pass the order paper, and the head of the woman is that of his wife, Effie. He went to the British Museum to search for information on tartans. He had difficulties in the composition of the group, wanting it to appear as one united body. The woman's hand, stretching round behind the soldier's back, helps keep them close together. The family and the scarlet-coated soldier are seen against a somber background.

Symbols in a story

The painting has a historic theme. The Scottish soldier is one of Bonnie Prince Charlie's men, imprisoned by the English. His wife has somehow obtained the order for his release, and he can go free. The sleeping child, heavy in her arms, may represent her long struggle; the dead flowers, the fading hopes of Bonnie Prince Charlie and his followers. The primroses, spring flowers, emphasize the age of the baby. Is there joy on the woman's face, or is she too tired to celebrate? The dog represents her faithfulness as well as its own delight at seeing its master again.

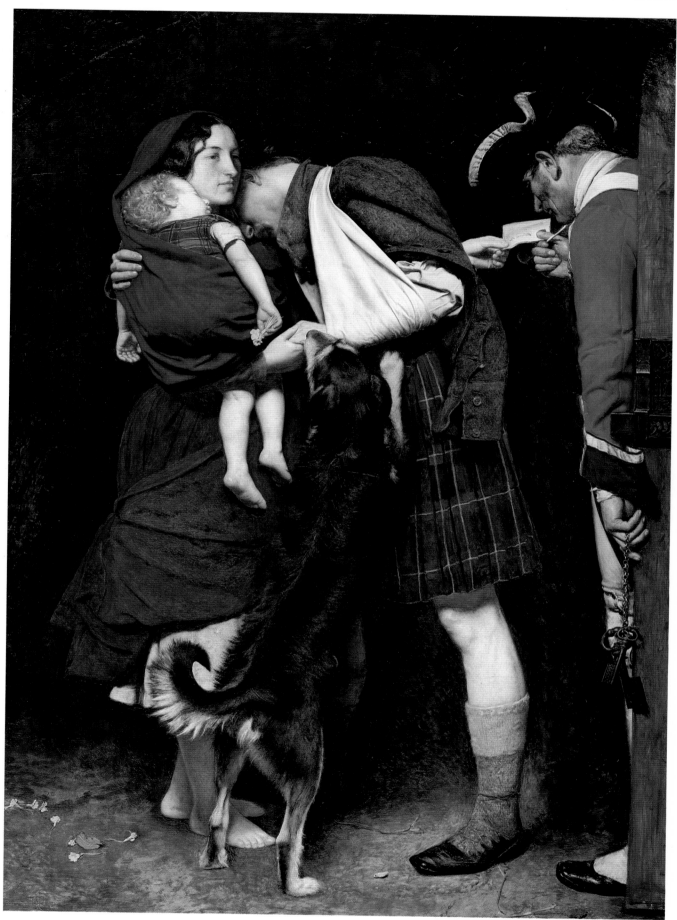

31

A Family Group in a Landscape

Oil on canvas 4'10¾" × 8'2¾"

Frans Hals

LIVED:
1581/5-1666

NATIONALITY:
Dutch

TYPE OF WORK:
oil paintings, especially portraits

The Metropolitan Museum of Art, New York. Bequest of Michael Friedsam 1931. The Friedsam Collection

Frans Hals led a troubled life. He gained a reputation as an excellent portrait painter but he was extravagant and he always had financial problems. His family were sometimes in trouble due to their boisterous behavior and Hals was too fond of drinking. He married twice, outliving both wives, and had ten children. Five of his sons became painters, but none rivaled their father's fame.

An ordinary beginning

Hals was probably taught to paint in Haarlem, in what is now The Netherlands, but few of his early paintings survive. His earliest known works are fairly ordinary portraits. They give no hint of the skill with which he was to paint a life-size group portrait of army officers in 1616. That painting made his name. It demonstrated his ability as a portrait painter, able to catch the character of individuals. It also showed his ability to compose figures into a group, capturing the atmosphere of the time and place.

No pretension

This painting is a family portrait of citizens of Haarlem. The silk and lace of their clothing suggests that they are wealthy, but they are not elegant aristocrats. Hals has made no attempt to make them into beautiful people. He has painted them as they are. In the children especially we see Hals's skill at informal portraits. The little girl in front looks up out of the picture as she feels for something in her basket. In a moment she might look down to see what she has found.

Hals has seen a family likeness in the group. In the women's faces, we see the same face in different stages of aging. The father, the baby on the left, and the little girl with the basket all have the same wide dark eyes.

Another artist

Hals painted the family in this picture, but the landscape behind them was done by another artist, probably a painter from Hals's studio or an artist hired to do such work for him. This was a common practice. The less important parts of a painting were often done by apprentices or less popular painters.

Dundee Art Galleries and Museums

Some Ideas

For lovers of people

You may have read this book because you like people. If so, perhaps you might try drawing the people in your own family so that you can get to know them better. Remember Gainsborough painting the portrait of his daughters? Looking at people with a painter's eyes could help you find out much more about the people around you.

For picture lovers

You may have read this book because you like looking at pictures. If so, perhaps you would like to see the original works. Remember how van Gogh got to know the painters of his time when he worked in a gallery? A list at the front of this book tells you where to find those paintings that are on view to the public. These paintings are in collections all over the world so you will not be able to see them all. Your nearest gallery may have other works by the artists you like.

For those who want to be artists

You may have read this book because you like to draw or paint. If so, perhaps it has helped you discover some of the secrets of picture-making. All the work that is in the book is the result of hard thinking, lots of practice, and above all — very careful looking. Remember the drawings of Leonardo and Raphael. They filled thousands of pages with their observations. Perhaps you could start a notebook now of local places and people, and work that goes on around you, and collect the information that will help you to make your ideas come alive.